Dirty Rotten

RULERS

HISTORY'S VILLAINS & THEIR
DASTARDLY DEEDS

Jim Pipe

Illustrated by Mauro Mazzara

Ticktock

An Hachette UK Company

www.hachette.co.uk

First published in the USA in 2014 by Ticktock,
an imprint of Octopus Publishing Group Ltd
Endeavour House 189 Shaftesbury Avenue
London
WC2H 8JY

www.octopusbooks.co.uk
www.octopusbooksusa.com
www.ticktockbooks.com

Distributed in the US by
Hachette Book Group USA
237 Park Avenue
New York NY 10017, USA

Distributed in Canada by
Canadian Manda Group
664 Annette Street
Toronto, Ontario, Canada M6S 2C8

ISBN 978 1 78325 163 6

Printed and bound in China

1 3 5 7 9 10 8 6 4 2

Commissioning Editor: Anna Bowles Designer: Ceri Hurst
History Consultant: Dr Matthew Kilburn, University of Oxford
Publisher: Samantha Sweeney
Managing Editor: Karen Rigden
Production Controller: Sarah-Jayne Johnson

Contents

Why so Horrible? 4

Qin the Merciless 6

Wicked Warlords 8

Herod the (not so) Great 10

Family Misfortunes 12

Nero the Zero 14

Dinners and Losers 16

Cruel Caligula 18

Bad Apples 20

Atilla the Killer 22

Don't Mess with the Mongols 24

Inglorious Generals 26

Bad King John 28

Naughty Knights 30

Vlad the Impaler 32

Bats About Blood 34

Old Ironsides 36

Unholy Terrors 38

The Beastly Borgias 40

Great Gluttons 42

Horrid Henry 44

Batty Builders 46

Ivan the Terrible 48

Mad Monarchs 50

The Ice Queen 52

Screwy Princesses 54

Master of Terror! 56

Peculiar Presidents 58

Vom Queen 60

Glossary 62

Why so Horrible?

What is it about rulers—kings, emperors, and warlords—that makes so many of them rotten? Did power go to their heads? Sometimes their families wanted to retain power, even if they knew the next generation wasn't up to the job.

Bad Apples

Some rulers were rotten from the start. Caligula was Roman emperor for just four years (AD 37–41) but still managed to go down in history as Rome's most tyrannical ruler.

Gone to the Dark Side

Others began as much-loved monarchs but soon turned nasty. Once a popular young prince known for his intelligence, musical ability, and dancing skills, today Henry VIII, a king of England, is infamous for beheading two of his wives as well as for killing thousands of other people.

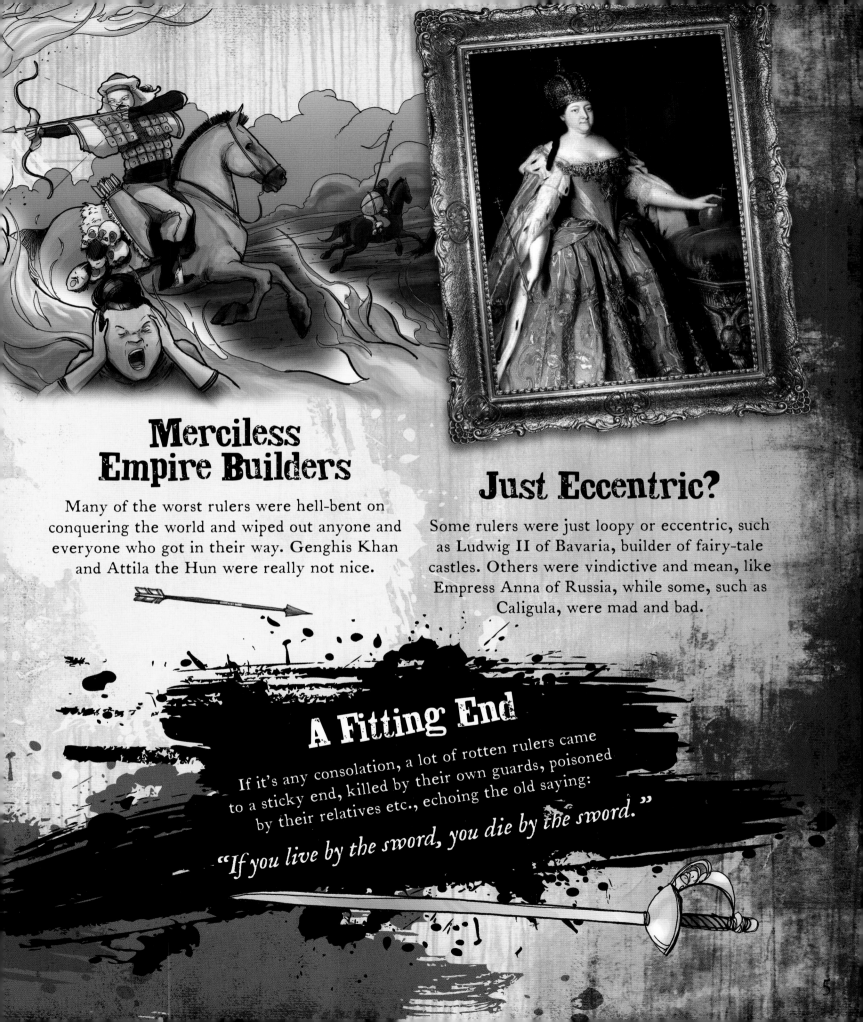

Merciless Empire Builders

Many of the worst rulers were hell-bent on conquering the world and wiped out anyone and everyone who got in their way. Genghis Khan and Attila the Hun were really not nice.

Just Eccentric?

Some rulers were just loopy or eccentric, such as Ludwig II of Bavaria, builder of fairy-tale castles. Others were vindictive and mean, like Empress Anna of Russia, while some, such as Caligula, were mad and bad.

A Fitting End

If it's any consolation, a lot of rotten rulers came to a sticky end, killed by their own guards, poisoned by their relatives etc., echoing the old saying:

"If you live by the sword, you die by the sword."

Qin the Merciless

China's first emperor, Qin Shi Huang, (259–210 BC) was bloodthirsty, brutal, and more than a little bonkers. Hundreds of thousands of people died building his pet projects.

A Death-Defying Plan

Qin came up with a cunning (some might say mad) plan to cheat death:

I

Order your scholars to brew a magical elixir (potion) that will make you live forever.

II

Send a fleet of ships to find Anqi Sheng. This 1,000-year-old wizard knows the secret to eternal life.

III

Never sleep in the same place twice.

IV

Always carry a massive crossbow at your side when traveling.

V

Build a maze of tunnels that allows you to sneak from one palace to another without being seen!

Blood, Sweat, and Tears

Emperor Qin forced a million laborers to work night and day. They built some 4,000 miles of roads and walls which eventually became the Great Wall of China.

Tomb Raiders

Qin Shi Huang constructed a huge underground tomb to protect him in death. Tens of thousands more workers died building it. The monument, discovered by farmers in 1974, still contains over 8,000 life-sized terracotta soldiers, along with thousands of bronze weapons to guard the emperor's tomb—or conquer heaven itself!

Goodbye, Qin!

Emperor Qin escaped several assassination attempts, including an attempt by a blind musician to bash him over the head with a lead lute (obviously a heavy metal fan). But in the end, he was killed by the very potions he hoped would make him live forever. They were laced with poisonous mercury!

Rotten Ruling

QIN'S DEADLY SINS:

☞ Slave driver

☞ Burying his scholars alive

☞ Playing with potions

7

Wicked Warlords

Forget not the words of the ancient sage:
"Silence is a friend who will never betray."
In other words, if there's a warlord about,
be very careful what you say at dinner!

Bandit Cannibals

In the 9th century, when warlord Huang Chao attacked the Chinese capital of Chang'an, he ordered his bandit army to "wash the city" with the blood of its 80,000 inhabitants. Thousands of victims were lined up and killed.

The Demon King

Japanese warlord Oda Nobunaga earned the nickname "the Demon King" after his attack on Mount Hiei in 1571. His troops burned 3,000 buildings to the ground, many of them temples and shrines.

Dong the Destroyer

Warlord Dong Zhuo rose from humble beginnings to become the most powerful man in China simply by killing anyone who stood in his way. Dong wiped out the entire Yuan clan after their leader fought against him, and then had thousands of officials executed in case they were still loyal to the emperor. To terrify his opponents, Dong Zhuo held lavish banquets. Captured enemies were the dish of the day.

Goodbye, Dong!

Eventually, Dong Zhuo was killed by his own bodyguard (in AD 192). A wick was lit on his belly, turning Dong's corpse into a human candle that burned for days (using his body fat as fuel).

Herod the (not so) Great

For someone whose rule brought 33 years of peace (37–4 BC), King Herod really has a rotten reputation. One Roman writer said: *"It's better to be Herod's pig than his son!"*

A Suspicious Mind

Herod persuaded the Romans to make him King of Judea (now Israel). But power went to his head and the kooky king became convinced that everyone was out to get him, including his favorite wife Mariamne.

Loves Me ...

On a visit to the Roman leader Octavian, Herod had a nasty feeling he was going to be assassinated. So he told his guards to kill Mariamne if he didn't return alive, as he couldn't bear the thought of someone else marrying her.

Loves Me NOT ...

Back home, Herod's sister Salome convinced him that Mariamne was plotting against him, and he had his beloved wife executed. Herod then had her body preserved in honey for seven years so he could still chat to her every day! The deranged king went on to wipe out most of his family.

Massacre of the Innocents

It didn't stop there. According to the Bible, in his quest to kill Jesus, Herod ordered the death of every boy aged 2 or under in the town of Bethlehem. There's no real proof this actually happened, but given how Herod treated his own family it could be true.

THE RUINS OF HEROD'S CITY, JERUSALEM

Goodbye, Herod!

Herod eventually died a horribly painful death at the age of 70: the softest parts of his body became infected and swelled up like a balloon. Just before he died, Herod ordered the execution of all the most important people in Judea, so everyone would be especially sad when they came to his funeral. Fortunately, this command was ignored.

Rotten Ruling

HEROD'S HEINOUS HORRORS:

☞ Massacring all the toddlers in a town

☞ Killing off members of his own family

☞ Pickling his wife. *Creepy!*

Family Misfortunes

King Herod wasn't the only rotten ruler to bump off his relatives.

An Ax to Grind

10th-century Viking warrior Eric Bloodax was the favorite, and probably the eldest, of the 20 sons of King Harald Finehair of Norway. Legend says that, to make sure he would be the next king, Eric murdered all of his brothers in turn.

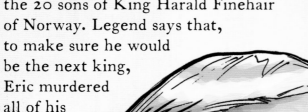

The Cage

In the 1500s, the Ottoman Empire was the most powerful state in the world. It had a special law to stop rival princes fighting over the throne when the old sultan (king) died. The new sultan had all his brothers executed, sometimes dozens of them at once, while nephews and cousins were locked up in a special jail known as the Kafes, or "cage."

Ouch!

King Edward II of England was found murdered in Berkeley Castle on September 21, 1327, after being captured and thrown into jail by his wife Queen Isabella and her lover Sir Roger Mortimer. A legend grew up that Edward had been killed by having a red-hot poker thrust into his rear.

The Wicked Uncle

English king Richard III is said to have murdered his two nephews in the Tower of London in 1483, shortly before grabbing the throne for himself. Two hundred years later, workmen at the Tower dug up a wooden box containing two small human skeletons, though it has never been proved that the bodies were the two princes.

Brotherly Love

In legend, twin brothers Romulus and Remus decided to build a city on the shores of the River Tiber in Italy. In a quarrel over where to start building, Romulus picked up a rock and killed his brother. Making himself king, he named the new city after himself: Rome.

Nero the Zero

Nero was a fat-bellied Roman emperor with a smelly body covered in spots. Power went to his head and he did some truly terrible things.

Mother Trouble

When Nero became emperor at just 16, his mother wanted to take charge instead of him, but Nero was determined to stop her. So he arranged for Agrippina to have a little accident. Or rather he tried to, because it took him three goes.

1) The sail of her boat was rigged to fall on her.
   (*Fail! It missed.*)

2) The crew sank the boat.
   (*Fail! Agrippina swam to shore.*)

3) Nero sent three assassins to finish her off.
   (*Success! Finally ...*)

NAME: Nero Claudius Caesar Augustus Germanicus
BORN: December 15, AD 37
DIED: June 9, AD 68
REIGNED: AD 54–68

Great Fire of Rome

In July AD 64, a fire broke out in Rome. Much of the wooden city quickly burned to ash. Nobody knows for certain, but many people thought Nero had started the fire to clear the land so he could build a grand house in the middle of the city. It was even said Nero sang while watching the fire from a distance.

Nero said the city's Christians were to blame for the fire. Nobody dared disagree with the emperor, so many Christians were rounded up and put to death horribly.

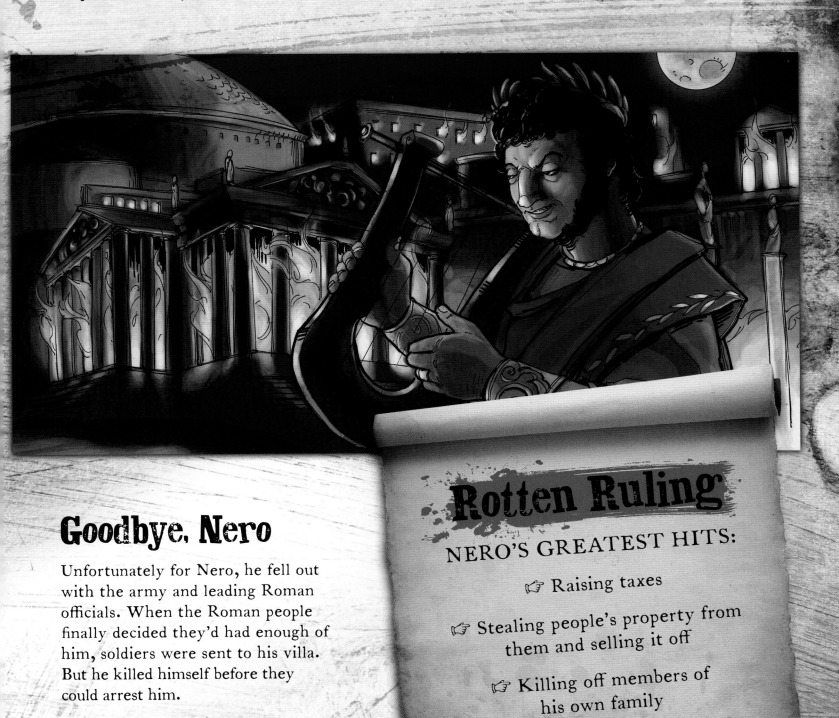

Goodbye, Nero

Unfortunately for Nero, he fell out with the army and leading Roman officials. When the Roman people finally decided they'd had enough of him, soldiers were sent to his villa. But he killed himself before they could arrest him.

Rotten Ruling

NERO'S GREATEST HITS:

☞ Raising taxes

☞ Stealing people's property from them and selling it off

☞ Killing off members of his own family

Dinners and Losers

Ancient Rome had more than its fair share of bad eggs,
from gladiator fanboys to creepy dinner hosts.

Dom's Fright Night

One night during the reign of Emperor Domitian (AD 81–96), dinner
guests were led to a black room lit only by flickering funeral candles.

☞ Servants were painted black from head to toe, and carried food dyed black that was served on black plates.

☞ Each place at the table was marked with a gravestone engraved with the guest's name.

☞ When the ghoulish meal was over, the terrified guests assumed they would be bumped off by imperial assassins ... but were dropped safely home.

The Gladiator Emperor

Commodus (who reigned AD 180–192) loved gladiator shows so much he often joined in!

☞ He killed three elephants single-handed in the arena, beheaded an ostrich, then told the senators attending that they were next.

☞ Feeling bored, Commodus once ordered all the criminals and beggars in the city to be rounded up, thrown into the arena, and forced to hack one another to death with meat cleavers.

Deadly Dinners

No one dared to refuse an invitation to dine with Emperor Elagabalus (who reigned AD 218–222). At best, you might get a nasty scare. At worst, you might die horribly:

☞ Guests were forced to eat live parrots or wrestle with lions.

☞ Spiders were hidden in the salad; lion's dung lurked in the pastry.

☞ Poisonous snakes were thrown into the room. Elagabalus watched as you either died from snakebites or were trampled to death in the rush toward the exit.

☞ On one occasion, Elagabalus showered his guests with flower petals—enough to suffocate some of them.

Cruel Caligula

Though he ruled for just four years (AD 37–41), Gaius Caesar, better known as Caligula, has gone down in history as Rome's most tyrannical emperor.

Hairy Legs

Caligula was very tall, with a bald head, spindly legs, and a hairy body. Anyone who looked down on him as he passed by, or used the word "goat" in the same sentence as his name, risked death.

A Tale of Whoa!

Caligula insisted on being treated like a god: his statues were put up all over the empire and temples were built so people could worship him.

The emperor loved his horse, Incitatus, so much he gave him a marble stable, dressed him in purple blankets and collars of precious stones, and fed him oats with gold flakes. Dinner guests were invited to the palace in the horse's name.

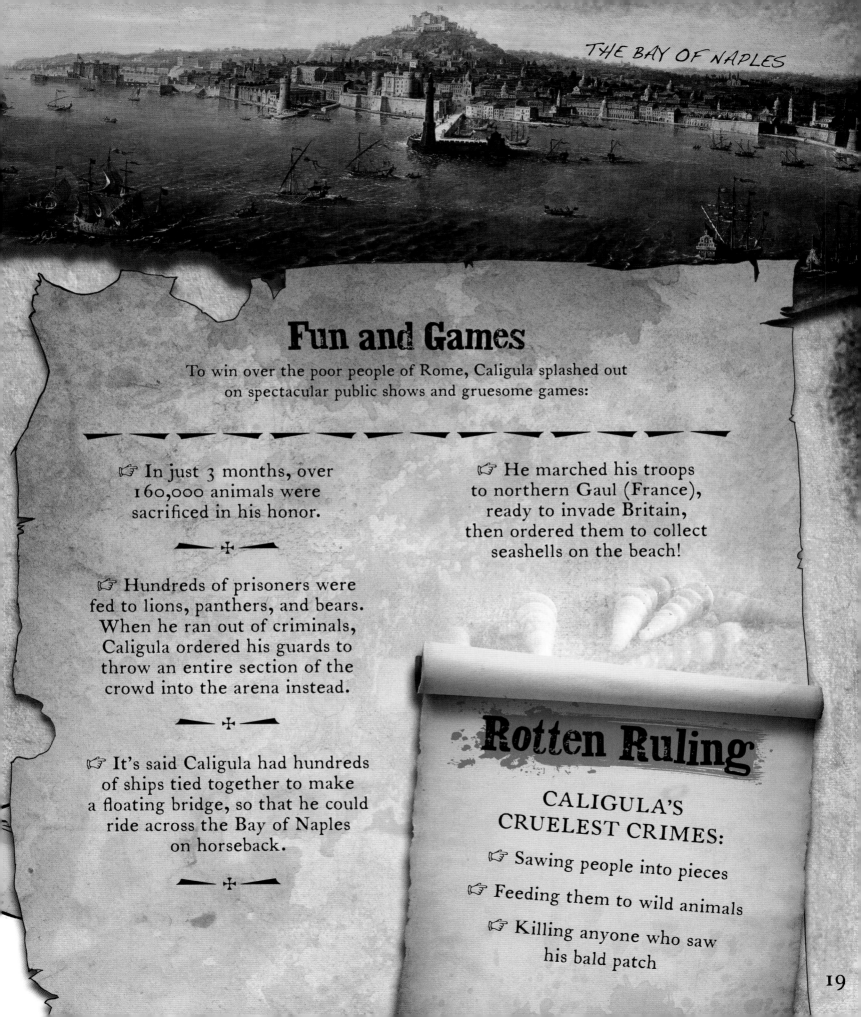

Fun and Games

To win over the poor people of Rome, Caligula splashed out
on spectacular public shows and gruesome games:

☞ In just 3 months, over 160,000 animals were sacrificed in his honor.

— ✢ —

☞ Hundreds of prisoners were fed to lions, panthers, and bears. When he ran out of criminals, Caligula ordered his guards to throw an entire section of the crowd into the arena instead.

— ✢ —

☞ It's said Caligula had hundreds of ships tied together to make a floating bridge, so that he could ride across the Bay of Naples on horseback.

— ✢ —

☞ He marched his troops to northern Gaul (France), ready to invade Britain, then ordered them to collect seashells on the beach!

Rotten Ruling

CALIGULA'S CRUELEST CRIMES:

☞ Sawing people into pieces

☞ Feeding them to wild animals

☞ Killing anyone who saw his bald patch

Bad Apples

Some rulers, such as England's Henry VIII, start off as confident, much-loved leaders, but as time goes by, go from bad to worse. Others, however, are rotten from the start ...

In a Snot?

French king Charles IX (1560–1574) was known as "The Snotty King," thanks to an ugly birthmark between his nose and upper lip. You can hardly blame him for that, but little Charles also loved torturing animals or whipping people until they bled.

Charles became king at the age of 13 (unlucky for some). Dominated by his mother, Catherine de' Medici, he ordered the murder of thousands of Protestants in the Saint Bartholomew's Day Massacre in 1572.

The Cruel Prankster

As a child, Christian VII of Denmark (1749–1808) stalked the streets of Copenhagen armed with a medieval spiked club, which he used to whack passersby. He played leapfrog over the backs of visiting diplomats when they bowed to him, or slapped them in the face without warning. Most strangely, he built his own rack to torture his best friend at court, then, to show how tough he was, burned his own flesh and rubbed salt into the wounds.

The King of Make-Believe

Zhengde became emperor of China in 1505 at the age of 14, and as far as anyone could tell, remained 14 for the rest of his 16-year reign. More than anything, Zhengde loved playing games of make-believe. He built a fake city block inside the palace grounds, then ordered his puzzled ministers to dress up and act as merchants while he played at being shopkeeper. He then ordered the release of a rebel leader, so he could experience the thrill of being a general and capturing the rebel himself.

Attila the Killer

Attila the Hun (AD 434–453), a very famous barbarian leader who attacked the Roman Empire, was nicknamed "the scourge" (after a horribly painful whip). Here's why:

The Huns galloped screaming and wailing into battle, with bloody heads and skulls tied to their saddles. *Yikes!*

After each victory, his men laid waste to neighboring towns. In Gaul (now France), the Huns reduced over 70 cities to smoking rubble.

When Attila met Saint Ursula, he wanted to marry her. Unwisely, she refused. Attila promptly had her killed, along with 11,000 of her companions.

He also ate two of his sons and killed his brother.

THE SCARE TACTICS WORKED

Theodosius II, ruler of Rome's Eastern Empire, paid Attila over 2 tons of gold (almost $85m today) not to attack his empire.

Note to Self:

Wipe out the Roman Empire

Be very, very scary!

Scorn or Mercy?

After the Romans sent an assassin to kill him, Attila asked him what his fee was. "50 pounds of gold," stammered the man. Attila gave the assassin 50 pounds of gold himself and told him to walk back home in disgrace.

Goodbye, Attila

In AD 453, the aged warlord and his latest young bride retired to their chamber on their wedding night. The next day, Attila the Hun's dead body was found covered in blood. Did he choke on a heavy nosebleed, or was he murdered by his bride? No one knows …

Rotten Ruling

ATTILA'S AWFUL ATROCITIES:

☞ Burning countless cities to the ground

☞ Tearing his enemies apart with wild horses

☞ Eating his sons

Don't Mess with the Mongols!

Crawling with lice and stinking horribly, the mighty Mongol hordes swept across the great plains of Asia in the 1200s. Their leader, Genghis Khan, gave his enemies a simple choice: "Surrender or die!" These terror tactics worked—the khan (ruler) conquered the largest empire in history, stretching from the Pacific Ocean to Eastern Europe.

Wiped Out!

The Mongols destroyed anyone who stood in their way, including a Persian tribe known as the Khwarezmids, who foolishly upset Genghis by beheading his messenger and shaving his ambassadors' heads. Bad move ...

☞ The Mongols attacked the Khwarezmid cities by catapulting diseased corpses over the walls to infect the people inside.

☞ Anyone left alive was put to the sword. Not even dogs or cats were spared.

☞ Farms with their crops were burned to the ground to starve any survivors.

☞ Genghis's men even changed the course of rivers, creating floods that wiped the Khwarezmid sultan's birthplace off the map.

Rotten Ruling

GENGHIS'S GRUESOME DEEDS:

☞ Killing a fifth of the world's population

☞ Picking on cats and dogs

☞ Collecting sacks of ears

What an earful!

The Mongols wiped out so many people that new forests sprang up where once there had been farms and villages. Many cities were so completely destroyed they were never rebuilt.

To count up all the bodies, the Mongols sometimes sliced an ear off each dead enemy and sent them back to Genghis as proof of their victory. After the Battle of Liegnitz in Poland in 1241, they collected nine large sacks of ears!

Inglorious Generals

Genghis Khan was just the worst of a very bad bunch.
History is filled with merciless generals who happily
wiped out their own men as well as their opponents!

A Pyramid of Skulls

King Timur (1336–1405) ruled
a tribe of warlike nomads based in
what is now Uzbekistan. Nicknamed
"the lame" because he walked with
a limp, Timur led his army on a
bloody rampage through Central Asia,
resulting in the deaths of some 17
million people. Timur had gigantic
pyramids of human skulls built outside
the towns he had destroyed.

Mommy's Boy?

Between 1810 and 1828, the Zulu
kingdom under Shaka Zulu conquered
large areas of what is now South Africa
and Zimbabwe. Like Genghis Khan,
Shaka ordered his soldiers to wipe out
his opponents, killing some 1 million
prisoners. But the cruel king had a
soft spot: his mom. When she died,
he ordered his men to kill anyone
who didn't seem sad enough.

Gold Crazy

During the Spanish conquest of America in the 16th century, soldiers such as Lope de Aguirre, nicknamed "El Loco" (the madman), slashed their way across the New World in a search for the legendary El Dorado, "the land of gold," all the while fighting angry local tribes, hunger, and disease. Desperate for riches and glory, they often wiped out whole villages. All this sent Aguirre mad, and he began murdering his own soldiers.

Adios, Brave Leg!

Antonio Lopez de Santa Anna was a Mexican generalissimo who only cared about himself.

In 1836, when his men stormed the Alamo fortress, he told his men to kill all the Texan defenders inside. He then laughed off his own huge losses in the bloody battle, saying: "What are the lives of soldiers but so many chickens?" But when he lost his leg in another battle, he ordered it to be buried with full military honors!

Bad King John

In the legend of Robin Hood, King John of England is the classic villain: greedy, violent, cruel, and ruthless. But was he really such a rotten ruler? In a word, **yes!**

» Weak «

John made a complete mess of being king. He faced a huge rebellion by the barons, fell out with the Pope, and he also lost many of the possessions he inherited, in particular large areas of land in France. After he failed to put down a revolt in northern France, the barons gave him the nickname "John Softsword."

» Untrustworthy «

John tried to snatch the throne (with the help of the French king), while his brother King Richard I was in jail abroad, losing the trust of the people even before he became king.

» Violent «

John imprisoned and killed anyone who threatened him, most famously his nephew, Arthur of Brittany. He also hanged 28 hostages, the sons of rebel Welsh chieftains.

» Ruthless «

John seduced the wives and daughters of his friends and enemies then banished their relatives so he could grab their land.

» Greedy «

John's favorite hobby was collecting jewelry. After bankrupting the county in a disastrous war with France, John tried to steal as much money as possible from his people by increasing taxes to record levels.

» Dishonest «

When the English barons threatened to rebel, he reluctantly signed the Magna Carta in 1215, then shamelessly went back on his word and fought back against his enemies.

So much for greed

John lost all his treasure when he got caught by the rising tide while taking a shortcut across a stretch of water in the Wash, Lincolnshire.

Rotten Ruling

JOHN'S BIGGEST MESSES:

☞ Losing almost all English lands in France

☞ Trying to steal the throne from his brother

☞ Losing his treasure

Naughty Knights

In legend, the Knights of the Round Table were brave, honest, and merciful. Sadly, real knights in the Middle Ages were not always so honorable.

Stripped for Action

Godfrey of Bouillon was a leader of the First Crusade, a military expedition by Christians in Europe to reconquer the Holy Lands (a part of the Middle East that is now several countries). Incredibly strong, it's said Godfrey once beheaded a camel with a single sword stroke! In 1099, his army reached Jerusalem. They charged into the city, killing everyone in sight. All that gore (and the hot sun) went to Godfrey's head: he stripped to his undergarments and walked barefoot through the bloody streets.

Gone to the Dark Side

The year was 1370, and the Hundred Years War between England and France was in full swing. Edward, an English prince and the most famous knight in Europe, was besieging the French town of Limoges. When it finally fell after several months, the so-called Black Prince was so furious it had held out so long he ordered his men to massacre the 3,000 unarmed men, women, and children who had surrendered to him.

The One-Eyed Dragon

In Japan, knights known as samurai followed a strict code—unless you were Date Masamune, a ruthless and bad-tempered warrior known as "the one-eyed dragon." As a young boy, he supposedly plucked out his own eye after it was damaged by smallpox (a deadly disease).

Masumune, who lived from 1567–1636, became one of the most feared knights in Japan. He was so violent toward his neighbors that a local lord tried to stop him by kidnapping his father. In the "rescue" attempt, Masamune simply killed his father along with all the kidnappers, their families, family pets, and anyone else nearby.

Vlad the Impaler

The word "vampire" is sometimes used to describe real people who carry out terrible crimes. There's no better example than Vlad III. On St. Bartholomew's Day in 1459 the cruel Prince of Wallachia had 30,000 men stuck on spikes while he set up a picnic table and scoffed his lunch, surrounded by a forest of corpses.

Son of a Dragon

A group of knights in Eastern Europe created the Order of the Dragon to fight against the Turks. When Vlad III's father joined the Order, he put their symbol—a dragon—on his coins. Vlad copied his father and became known as Dracula, or "the son of the dragon." The prince's bloody reputation inspired Irish writer Bram Stoker when he created the world's most famous storybook vampire.

Vlad the Impaler

Vlad was so fond of sticking his enemies on spikes he is known as Vlad the Impaler. Temporarily imprisoned by the king of Hungary, he passed the time catching birds and mice and sticking them on tiny spears.

In one story, two ambassadors from a nearby kingdom refused to take off their hats during a visit to Vlad's castle. The prince ordered his men to nail the hats to their heads, so the men would never have to take them off again.

Goodbye Dracula

Vlad Dracula was killed in battle against the Turks in 1476. His head was cut off and sent to the Turkish capital Constantinople, where the sultan had it stuck on a stake to show that the Impaler was finally dead.

Rotten Ruling

VLAD'S VICIOUSNESS:

☞ Impaling his enemies on spikes

☞ Nailing hats to heads

☞ Making a forest of corpses

Bats About Blood

Vlad Dracula and Attila the Hun deliberately spread stories about how horrible they were, knowing it would strike fear into their enemies. Other rotten rulers sacrificed their prisoners to keep their gods happy, while one used her victims' blood as a bizarre beauty treatment!

Feeding the Sun

In the 1400s, the Aztecs ruled over much of what is now Mexico. To honor their gods, they often slaughtered large numbers of captured prisoners. In 1487, King Ahuitzotl set a new record when he spent four days killing 20,000 victims to celebrate his new temple at Tenochtitlán. As the captives were marched up to the altar, priests and Aztec nobles, including Ahuitzotl, cut out their hearts. They believed this would allow the victims' hearts to fly up to the Sun and feed it with energy.

Head Business

In the 1800s, the kings of Dahomey (now Benin in West Africa) honored their dead ancestors by chopping the heads off dozens of slaves and war captives. In the local Fon language, the ceremony's name—*Xwetanu*—meant "yearly head business."

The Bloody Countess

Erzsebet Bathory (who lived from 1560–1614) was a Hungarian countess who thought that taking a bath in the blood of girls would keep her young and beautiful. Her servants lured girls to her castle, where they were murdered. Eventually the truth came out when locals became suspicious about the missing girls. Some reports say that as many as 600 victims helped to keep the countess's bath topped up.

Goodbye, Countess

In 1610, Countess Bathory was locked up in her bedroom as a punishment and fed through a tiny slot in the wall. She died four years later.

Old Ironsides

Some 450 years after Oliver Cromwell went to Ireland, the town of Drogheda still has a road that remembers his dirty deeds—Scarlett Lane—for all the blood that once flowed down its streets.

The Bogeyman

In 1649, Parliamentary forces defeated King Charles I and beheaded him after winning the English Civil War. Their leader, Oliver Cromwell, then brought an army to Ireland to stamp out support for the royal family.

As a Puritan (a strict Protestant), Cromwell also wanted to crush the Catholic Church. His soldiers showed no mercy, slaughtering hundreds and forcing thousands of Irish families from their homes. Cromwell gained such a reputation for cruelty that for centuries to come, Irish mothers threatened children with: "Eat up or Cromwell will get you."

The Sack of Drogheda

Cromwell, nicknamed "Old Ironsides" for his toughness, launched a savage attack on the town of Drogheda. The defenders of St. Peter's Church were roasted alive, while the commander of the town was beaten to death with his own wooden leg! Cromwell's men then stuck the heads of Drogheda's leaders on pikes and sold the survivors to slave plantations in the Caribbean.

Fire and Water

The town of Wexford was next. Here five priests were burned at the stake and their bodies flung into the sewers. And at Bishop's Rock in Inishbofin, off the coast of Connemara, a priest was tied to a rock and his colleagues were forced to watch as he drowned in the rising tide.

Rotten Ruling

CROMWELL'S CRUELEST CUTS:

☞ Slaughtering the townspeople of Wexford and Drogheda

☞ Burning priests at the stake

☞ Beating someone to death with his own leg

Goodbye Cromwell

Cromwell died peacefully in 1658 and was buried in Westminster Abbey. But when the Royalists returned to power in 1660 they dug up his corpse, cut off its head, and hung it in chains.

Unholy Terrors

During the period 1200–1600, rotten rulers all over Europe were targeting people for their beliefs. More often than not, these persecutions were an excuse to grab land and money.

Death to Innocents

In Spain, cruel-hearted Tomás de Torquemada rooted out "enemies" of the Catholic Church—many of them innocent Jews and Muslims. Suspects were tortured until they confessed to their alleged crimes.

During his 28 years in power, 1470–1498, over 2,000 people were burned to death. After being sentenced, the victims were forced to wear black clothes decorated with dragons and snakes.

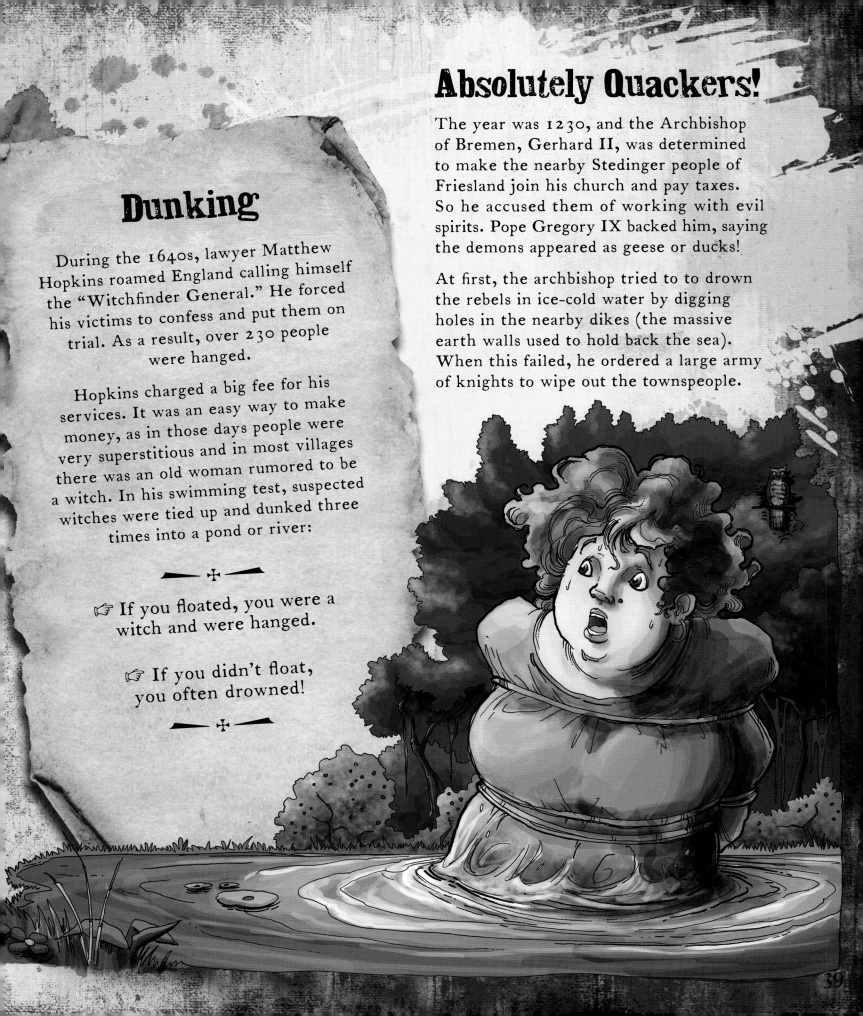

Dunking

During the 1640s, lawyer Matthew Hopkins roamed England calling himself the "Witchfinder General." He forced his victims to confess and put them on trial. As a result, over 230 people were hanged.

Hopkins charged a big fee for his services. It was an easy way to make money, as in those days people were very superstitious and in most villages there was an old woman rumored to be a witch. In his swimming test, suspected witches were tied up and dunked three times into a pond or river:

— ✠ —

☞ If you floated, you were a witch and were hanged.

☞ If you didn't float, you often drowned!

— ✠ —

Absolutely Quackers!

The year was 1230, and the Archbishop of Bremen, Gerhard II, was determined to make the nearby Stedinger people of Friesland join his church and pay taxes. So he accused them of working with evil spirits. Pope Gregory IX backed him, saying the demons appeared as geese or ducks!

At first, the archbishop tried to to drown the rebels in ice-cold water by digging holes in the nearby dikes (the massive earth walls used to hold back the sea). When this failed, he ordered a large army of knights to wipe out the townspeople.

The Beastly Borgias

The Borgias were a Spanish family famed for the murder and mayhem they brought to Rome in the mid-1400s. Their favorite party trick was invite wealthy victims to dinner and then poison them.

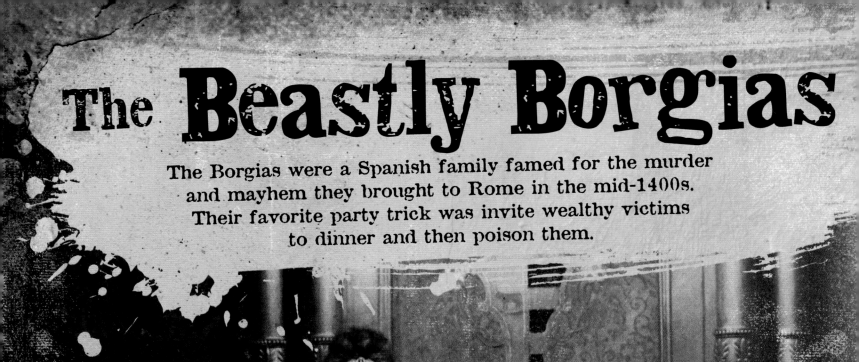

Meet the Mob

Rodrigo and his children wrongly accused nobles and church leaders of crimes. After flinging their rivals in jail or killing them, the Borgias grabbed all their property. The Venetian ambassador reported: "Every night four or five men are discovered assassinated, bishops and others, so that all Rome trembles for fear of being murdered."

RODRIGO
» the Big Boss «

Rodrigo Borgia was elected Pope Alexander VI in 1492, after buying most of the votes. The fun-loving pope then busied himself with lavish banquets, plays, and dance parties—all paid for with the money looted from the Church or stolen from his rivals.

LUCREZIA
» the Poisoner «

Rodrigo's teenage daughter Lucrezia had a ring that was hollowed out in the middle and contained a dose of poison. Poisoning was all the rage in those times. Textbooks were written describing how to make the perfect poison.

CESARE
» the Murderer «

The most ruthless of Rodrigo's children was Cesare, who killed anyone who got in his way, including his elder brother, Giovanni, whose body was found floating in the Tiber River. He also ordered his men to strangle his sister Lucrezia's second husband.

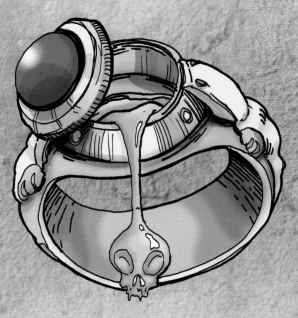

Rotten Ruling

BORGIA BEASTLINESS:

☞ Poisoning dinner guests

☞ Murdering friends and family

☞ Committing robbery and bribery

Goodbye Rodrigo

In 1503, Alexander fell ill. So did Cesare, and a rumor grew in Rome that they had both been poisoned after Cardinal Adrian Corneto switched the poison cup that Cesare had prepared for him. Within a few days, Cesare recovered, but his father died.

Great Gluttons

You can definitely have too much of a good thing, especially when it comes to food. King Adolf Fredrik of Sweden (who reigned from 1751–1771) is still known to schoolchildren there as "the king who ate himself to death" after eating 14 servings of his favorite dessert at the end of a big meal.

Food, Glorious Food!

The Roman Emperor Vitellius feasted three or four times a day. He often vomited after his meals, using a long feather to stick down his throat, so he could eat more food. In one banquet alone, guests gobbled down 2,000 fish and 7,000 birds!

Vitellius loved unusual treats, such as pheasants' brains and flamingoes' tongues, and ordered his navy to search far and wide for rare ingredients.

The Big Eater

In a typical day, Henry VIII ate 13 different dishes. In one year, the English king and his guests ate 8,200 sheep, 2,330 deer, 2,870 pigs, 1,240 oxen, 24,000 larks, and 33,000 chickens!

Princess Chubby

Princess Marie Louise of Orléans, France (who lived from 1695–1719), nicknamed "Princess Chubby" by her friends, just didn't know when to stop eating. As soon as she woke, servants rushed to her room with a selection of treats. She got up at 12 o'clock then ate until 3:00 p.m. An hour later at 4 o'clock, fruit, cream, and salads were served to her.

In 1718, she gave a famous ball where dozens of courses were served, including 32 types of soup, 370 partridges and pheasants, and 100 baskets of fresh fruit. After stuffing herself silly one night at an open-air banquet, the princess caught a chill and died, aged just 23.

Piggy President

US president Zachary Taylor loved nothing better than wolfing down iced milk and cherries. In 1850, he tucked into bowlfuls of the dessert during while celebrating Independence Day. Falling ill later that night, he died five days later.

Horrid Henry

English king Henry VIII (1509–1547) was a bloodthirsty tyrant best known for marrying six times. The popular rhyme *"Divorced, Beheaded, Died, Divorced, Beheaded, Survived"* tells what happened to his wives!

The Six Wives

1 Catherine of Aragon got on well with the king, but when they failed to have a son, he divorced her.

4 Anne of Cleves was picked out by Henry's minister Thomas Cromwell. Henry complained of her ugliness and "evil smells," but once they were divorced, she became good friends with the king.

2 Anne Boleyn had been a lady-in-waiting to Catherine. But when she too failed to give Henry a son, he had her beheaded, accusing Anne of falling in love with someone else—and being a witch (she had six fingers on one hand)!

5 Catherine Howard was Anne of Cleves's maid of honor. Two years later, she was beheaded after Henry found out she was having an affair.

3 Jane Seymour was lady-in-waiting to both Catherine and Anne. She gave the king a son, but died soon after the birth.

6 Catherine Parr was a loving stepmother to Henry's children and the only wife to survive him.

From Hero to Horror

Young Henry was tall and handsome, a fine musician, and a skilled archer, wrestler, and tennis player. But as his reign continued, he executed some 72,000 English subjects. Louis Perreau, the French ambassador to England, called him "the most dangerous and cruel man in the world."

Henry Blows It

When a jousting accident stopped him from exercising, Henry ballooned to nearly 322 pounds and developed horrible sores all over his body. He died a slow, painful death in bed, and it's said that a few days later his horribly bloated corpse exploded in the coffin!

Rotten Ruling

HENRY'S HORRID HITS:

☞ Chopping the heads off two of his wives

☞ Executing thousands of other people

☞ Eating himself silly every day

Batty Builders

Henry VIII built one palace after another to show how incredibly important he was. By the end of his reign, he had almost 60! Other really rotten rulers constructed towering temples and fairy-tale castles.

Reach for the Sky!

If you're an Egyptian pharaoh, how do you live forever? Just build a pyramid.

☞ This massive tomb acts like a gigantic stairway, helping your soul on its way to the heavens when you die. *Awesome!*

☞ Don't worry, the hard work is done by thousands of Egyptian peasants, who lay around 300 stones a day.

☞ Legend has it that when Napoleon visited the great pyramids at Giza over 2,000 years later, he calculated that there was enough stone in the pyramids to build a 10-foot-high wall around France.

Temples of Blood

Mayan kings built giant temples to worship the gods. Here they offered their own blood as a sacrifice. They jabbed spines through their ear or drew strings of thorns through their tongue! On important feast days, captured enemies were sacrificed.

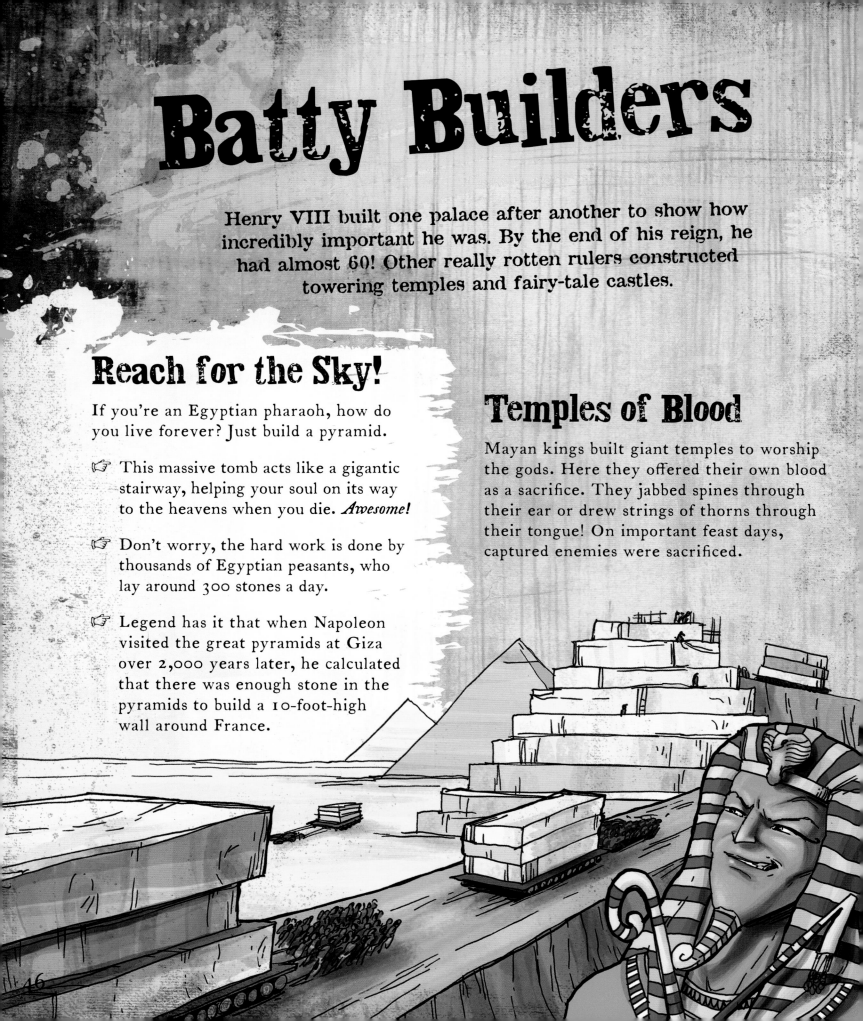

Fantasy Farm

To escape from court life, French queen Marie Antoinette had a peasant village built in the grounds of the Palace of Versailles. She would invite friends here for fresh berries and ice cream. It was a real working farm, supplying crops and meat to the palace kitchens. Even after the queen was put in jail by revolutionaries in 1792, she had fresh milk and other goods delivered to her from the farm.

The Fairy-Tale King

Ludwig II of Bavaria is best remembered for building Neuschwanstein, a fairy-tale castle perched on a mountaintop. One room was like a fairy grotto, with its own waterfall!

Ivan the Terrible

A deeply religious man and a great scholar, Ivan IV of Russia (who lived from 1530–1584) was a larger-than-life character who drank too much, laughed too loudly, and never forgot anything. But his terrible mood swings turned him into a savage ruler who lived up to his legendary name, "Ivan the Terrible."

Flying Fur

Ivan was cruel even as a child, perhaps because he was caught up in a violent family feud. He threw dogs and cats from the walls of the Kremlin palace, and roamed the streets of Moscow with a gang of young thugs, knocking down old people for fun. At 13, he ordered the arrest of a rival prince, who was thrown to a pack of starving dogs.

Spy Network

When his wife Anastasia died, Ivan was sure she had been poisoned. Fearing that assassins lurked around every corner, he created a secret police force. They dressed in black, rode black horses, and their saddles were marked with a dog's head and broom—symbols of their mission to sniff out treason and sweep it away.

Rule of Terror

In 1570, Ivan believed the entire town of Novgorod was plotting to overthrow him. Ivan led the attack himself, and 60,000 people were slaughtered. One rich landowner was strapped to a barrel of gunpowder and blown to pieces.

In a rage, he beat his own son to death with a walking cane, and killed one of his wives the day after they got married.

It's also said that he had the architects of St. Basil's cathedral blinded, after he feared they might build another more beautiful cathedral elsewhere.

Rotten Ruling

IVAN'S MOST TERRIBLE CRIMES:

☞ Slaughtering the town of Novgorod

☞ Beating his own son to death

☞ Throwing cats and dogs from the palace walls

Mad Monarchs

Though most really rotten rulers weren't as destructive and terrifying as Ivan the Terrible, you probably wouldn't want to share a palace with any of this lot ...

Justin the Biter

Hearing voices in his head, the Byzantine emperor Justin II (who reigned from AD 565–574) used to hide under his bed. He also had a habit of biting his servants, and it was even whispered that he ate two of them. His servants did their best to drown out the voices by playing loud organ music. They also distracted the emperor by pushing him around the palace in a throne on wheels.

Princely Potshots

In the 1200s, Mansa (Emperor) Khalifa of Mali amused himself by standing on the palace roof and shooting arrows at passersby. This wasn't such a hit with everyone else and Khalifa was murdered just a year after he became king.

Six hundred years later, King Otto of Bavaria liked to start his day by shooting at workers in the royal gardens. To prevent casualties, his servants handed him a rifle loaded with blanks, then played dead when he shot at them.

Breaking News!

One hot August day in 1392, French king Charles VI was riding through a forest when the sound of a lance being dropped made him fly into such a rage that he killed four of his own knights. The royal doctors tried to cure the king by drilling holes in his head, but he only got worse. Believing he was made of glass, Charles wouldn't let anyone near him in case he broke into pieces. He even had iron rods put in his clothes to stop his bones from breaking.

What a pane!

The Rice Box Prince

Crown Prince Sado of Korea (who lived from 1735–1762) liked to murder a few servants every day. To put a stop to the slaughter, his father (the king) ordered Sado to climb into a rice chest. The chest was nailed shut and Sado died eight days later.

The Ice Queen

In 1740, Europe suffered its worst winter for 30 years. What else was there for a bored empress to do but build a palace made completely of ice?

Secret Police

Anna Ivanovna, empress of Russia from 1730–1740, was a tough cookie. She had been made empress by a group of powerful nobles who expected her to follow their orders. But Anna dismissed the nobles from court and created a new secret police force, famed for slitting the noses of her enemies.

A Palace of Ice

Mean Anna loved making members of her court look stupid. Most famously, she forced a prince who had angered her to marry an ugly serving maid, then set about building a spectacular palace of ice for the wedding.

☞ Huge blocks of ice were "glued" together with water, which froze instantly.

☞ In the bedroom, sculptors carved a bed with four bedposts and a canopy, pillows, and a mattress from ice.

☞ In the garden, they carved ice birds sitting in ice trees, while a life-sized ice elephant spouted water from its trunk during the day and fire at night. Inside, a trumpeter made it roar!

☞ Six cannons were also sculpted from solid ice, which could be fired with a small charge of gunpowder.

Anna did all this just to humiliate the prince. She ordered him and his new wife to dress as clowns then forced them to spend the night in the freezing ice palace without their clothes on! A large crowd was invited to watch.

Rotten Ruling

AWFUL ANNA'S
MEANEST MOMENTS:

☞ Slitting people's noses

☞ Trying to freeze Prince Mikhail Golitsyn and his wife to death

Goodbye Anna

When spring came, the ice palace melted. The spiteful empress died later that year from a painful illness. As for the prince and his new bride, they survived the night after she traded a pearl necklace with one of the guards for a sheepskin coat, and they lived happily ever after!

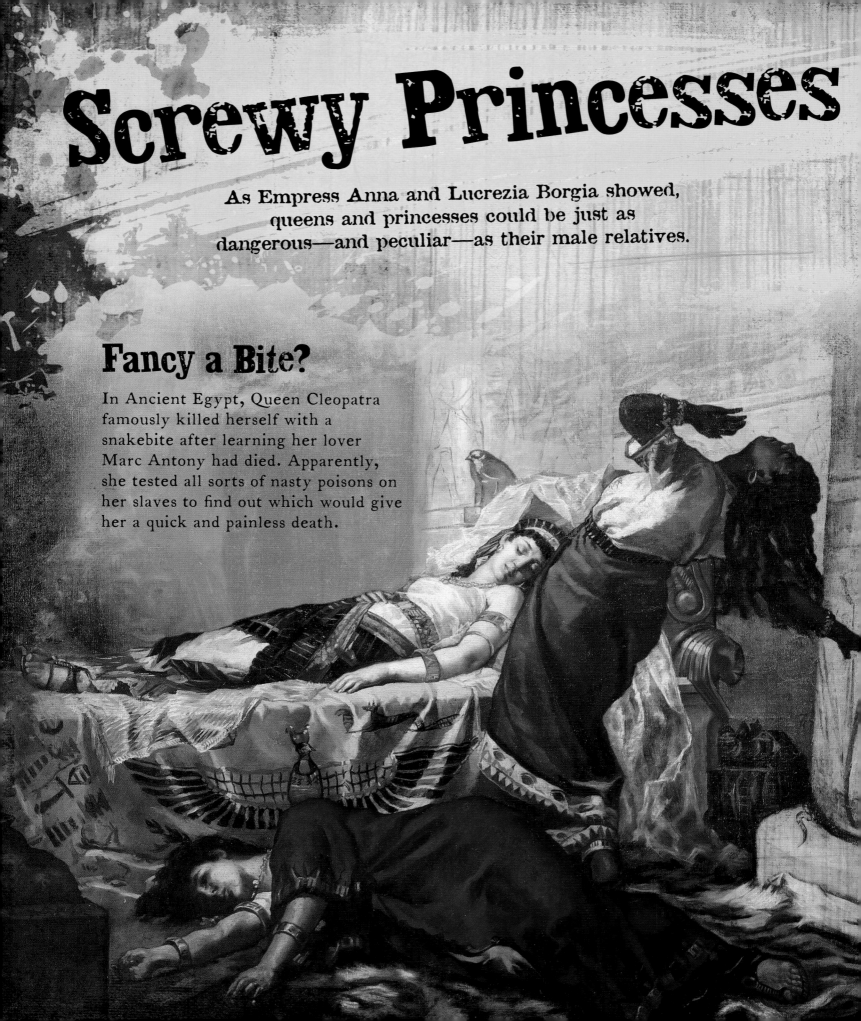

Screwy Princesses

As Empress Anna and Lucrezia Borgia showed,
queens and princesses could be just as
dangerous—and peculiar—as their male relatives.

Fancy a Bite?

In Ancient Egypt, Queen Cleopatra
famously killed herself with a
snakebite after learning her lover
Marc Antony had died. Apparently,
she tested all sorts of nasty poisons on
her slaves to find out which would give
her a quick and painless death.

Highly Strung

A 19th-century princess, Alexandra of Bavaria, had a thing for keeping clean—so much so that she insisted on wearing only spotless white clothes. Not so strange, but it gets worse. One day, she was seen walking sideways through the palace corridors. When asked why by her family, she told them that she had swallowed a glass grand piano and she was afraid of getting stuck.

A Final Kiss

Queen Juana of Castile was mad about her husband, Philip "the Handsome" of Austria. When he caught a fever and died in 1506, Juana had the coffin opened five weeks later to have a last look at her beloved's remains. After the wrappings were removed, Juana began kissing the corpse's feet so passionately that she had to be dragged away. From then on, wherever Juana went, so did the coffin.

Eccentric Empress

After Empress Carlota's husband was shot by a firing squad during the 1867 Mexican revolution, she grew more and more eccentric. In Rome, she burst into the Pope's apartments screaming that her staff had tried to poison her.

The next day, while visiting a convent, she snatched a piece of meat from a pan in the kitchen. She burned her hand, fainted from the pain, and was hurried off to her hotel room, where it was found she had a live chicken tied to the legs of a table.

Master of Terror!

Robespierre was the leader of the French Revolution. As a young lawyer, he had fought hard to protect the rights of ordinary people, but once in power, he ruled over "the terror," a period lasting about a year in which 300,000 people were arrested and 17,000 executed, including King Louis XVI and Queen Marie Antoinette.

Madame La Guillotine

Most victims of the terror had their heads chopped off by the guillotine, nicknamed the "national razor." The executions attracted large crowds; some people came day after day, including a group of women who worked on their knitting while the heads rolled.

Power Struggle

Robespierre only had to point a finger of suspicion and people were sent to the guillotine, accused of not supporting the French Revolution, hoarding, deserting the army, and a host of other crimes. In this way Robespierre eliminated many of his political opponents. He guillotined entire families of aristocrats and ordinary people. Most were killed without trial.

Vendée Massacre

Robespierre was also responsible for ordering the massacre of rebels in the Vendée region of France.

Over 150,000 people were killed. In the city of Nantes, the men, women, and children were tied together in boats that were towed out to the middle of the Loire River and then sunk.

The "Incorruptible"

Unusually, Robespierre did not use his power to make money or live extravagantly. He lived simply: walking everywhere, going for strolls in the country, and enjoying musical evenings with his landlord's family.

Adieu, Robespierre

"The terror" and Robespierre's lust for power made him unpopular. In 1794, Robespierre and 21 of his closest supporters were guillotined. The night before, he had tried to shoot himself, but only succeeded in shattering his jaw.

Rotten Ruling

ROBESPIERRE'S WRATH:

☞ Committing the brutal massacre in the Vendée region

☞ Sending thousands to the guillotine, including some of his friends

Peculiar Presidents

In North America, rebels broke from rule by England in 1776 and created a new nation, the United States of America. Though they got rid of one mad ruler, England's King George III, they ended up with a few eccentrics of their own!

Old Hickory

Before he became U.S. president in 1829, Andrew Jackson loved duels, which meant standing a few steps away from someone armed with a loaded pistol and shooting at them, while they in turn shot at you. He may have fought up to 100 of them.

Jackson kindly allowed one opponent, Charles Dickenson, the first shot. The bullet hit Jackson in the arm, and remained there for the next 19 years. But it didn't stop him from shooting back, killing Dickenson.

No Teddy Bear

Though teddy bears are named after U.S. president Theodore "Teddy" Roosevelt, he was no softie. A champion boxer, he could ride 100 miles in a day and walked around the White House with a pistol in his belt.

Shot by an assassin in 1912 as he got into his car, Roosevelt drove to his next appointment and told the stunned audience: "It takes more than that to kill a Bull Moose!" He then spoke for 80 minutes with a bullet hole in his chest!

Strange but True!

☞ When the first electric lights were put into the White House in 1891, President Benjamin Harrison and his wife were so terrified of getting an electric shock they often went to bed with the lights on.

— ✛ —

☞ President Calvin Coolidge apparently enjoyed having his head rubbed with petroleum jelly while eating his breakfast in bed.

— ✛ —

☞ President Jimmy Carter once claimed he had seen a UFO, saying:

"It was the darndest thing I've ever seen. It was big, it was very bright, it changed colors, and it was about the size of the moon."

Vom Queen

In the 1800s, ruthless Queen Ranavalona I put the "mad" into Madagascar, an island now known for its vanilla and cuddly cartoon animals.

Rise to Power

Born into a peasant family, Ranavalona got her lucky break when her father uncovered a plot to kill the Madagascan king, who gratefully married Ranavalona to his son. Surprise, surprise: the unlucky prince soon died in mysterious circumstances and Ranavalona wasted no time in bumping off the rest of the royal family.

By 1828, she was queen and supreme ruler. When French and British forces tried to take control, her forces beat them back. Ranavalona cut the heads off her dead enemies, stuck them on pikes, and lined them up along the beach as a warning.

A Sick Punishment

Under Ranavalona, anyone accused of a crime was forced to drink a poisonous juice made from the tangena plant, then fed three pieces of chicken skin. Those who failed to vomit up all three pieces were found guilty—if they hadn't already died from the poison, that is. As many as 100,000 people may have died in this way.

The Royal Bath

Once a year, Ranavalona took a bath on her balcony. People came from all over the island to watch. Afterward, she poured the bathwater over the spectators, anointing them like a god. Not very hygienic, but better than her treatment of local Christians, who were flung from cliffs or boiled in water.

Rotten Ruling

RANAVALONA'S VILEST VICES:

☞ Throwing Christians off cliffs

☞ Slaughtering the royal family

☞ Poisoning thousands of innocent victims

Goodbye Ranavalona

Unusually for a really rotten ruler, Ranavalona died peacefully in her bed at the age of 80, after reigning for 33 years.

Glossary

Abbey: a religious building that is home to monks or nuns

Ambassador: a person chosen to represent a foreign country or a particular activity, usually in another country

Archbishop: the head bishop who is in charge of a large area or district

Assassin: a person who deliberately kills an important figure, usually for religious or political reasons

Barbarian: a person considered savage and uncivilized

Baron: a member of the lowest rank of the British nobility

Bishop: an important member of the Christian Church. Bishops are usually in charge of a group of churches or whole area of lands

Cardinal: a leader of the Roman Catholic Church, appointed by the Pope

Catapult: a weapon used to launch large stones or other objects across long distances, often made from a lever and ropes

Crossbow: a large wooden weapon used in medieval times to fire arrows at enemies

Crusade: a military expedition by European Christians in the 11th, 12th, and 13th centuries. Crusades were usually carried out to try to gain back land in Israel from the Muslims

Emperor/empress: the male or female ruler of an empire

Generalissimo: the head of the army, navy, and air force in certain countries

Gladiator: a man (in Ancient Rome) who is trained to fight with weapons against other men or wild animals in an arena

Guillotine: a machine used in the French Revolution to chop off people's heads using a heavy blade that is dropped down between two wooden posts

Imperial: of or from an empire, emperor, or empress

Parliament: the group of people elected to respresent the people of a country and make its laws

Persecution: a campaign to kill, drive away, or control a group of people usually because of their religion, race, or beliefs

Pharaoh: the title of an Ancient Egyptian king. The pharaohs are famous for being made into mummies and buried in pyramids when they died

Pike: a weapon with a pointed end

Pope: the head of the Roman Catholic Church. The Pope lives in the Vatican City in Italy and is the world's most famous religious leader

Protestant: a Christian who does not follow the Catholic Church

Puritan: a strict Protestant. Puritans originated in the 16th century within the Church of England

Nomad: a person who moves around from place to place, usually as part of a tribe

Revolt: a rebellion against those who are in authority

Revolutionaries: people who take part in a revolution and try to overthrow the people in power such as parliament or the monarchy

Sage: a very wise person who others turn to for advice

Samurai: the military warriors of medieval Japan. They were known for being very violent

Senator: a member of the senate, a group of people with a lot of power within the ruling party of a country

Sultan: the ruler of an Islamic country

Tyrant/tyranny/tyrannical: a tyrant is a person in power who uses their power in an unfair and harsh (tyrannical) way

Vikings: Scandinavian pirates who robbed communities along the coasts of Europe from the 8th to the 10th centuries

Warlord: a military leader who has seized power (often in a violent manner), especially in one part of a country